One Line a Day Journal for Teens

One Line a Day Journal for Teens

A Day

Journal for Teens

▶ *Three Years of Daily Reflections and Memories*

ROCKRIDGE
PRESS

For general information on our other products and services or to obtain technical support, please contact our Customer Care Department within the United States at (866) 744-2665, or outside the United States at (510) 253-0500.

Rockridge Press publishes its books in a variety of electronic and print formats. Some content that appears in print may not be available in electronic books, and vice versa.

TRADEMARKS: Rockridge Press and the Rockridge Press logo are trademarks or registered trademarks of Callisto Media Inc. and/or its affiliates, in the United States and other countries, and may not be used without written permission. All other trademarks are the property of their respective owners. Rockridge Press is not associated with any product or vendor mentioned in this book.

Interior and Cover Designer: Gabe Nansen
Art Producer: Hannah Dickerson
Editor: Julie Haverkate
Production Editor: Dylan Julian
Production Manager: Eric Pier-Hocking

Alpha and Numeric Graphics © Darumo Shop/ Creative Market; All other illustrations used under license from Shutterstock.com

Paperback ISBN: 978-1-63878-082-3
R0

This Book Belongs To

....

Introduction

This journal is a place for you to record short yet notable thoughts and events—big or small—to look back on year after year and cherish forever. Down the line some might make you laugh, some might make you cringe or cry, but all these memories will be authentically YOURS forever.

The best part about this journal is that you can start any day or month of the year. No offense to January—you just don't know when you'll pick up this book. Let's say you start on April 9. Once you're on that page, you begin by recording the year at the top of that date's section. Then, use the first section to add your musings of the day: maybe something about family or friends, or a thought that made you feel something (proud, happy, sad, mad, thankful, and so on). It's really up to you. Move to the next day and do the same. Continue for the rest of the year; then, when the year has ended, move to the second space provided, and repeat for the third year. Eventually, you'll have memories and experiences to look back on, year after year. Happy journaling!

"THE MIRACLE ISN'T THAT I FINISHED. THE MIRACLE IS THAT I HAD THE COURAGE TO START."

—John Bingham

JAN
1

20___ ....

....

20___ ....

....

20___ ....

....

JAN
2

20___ ....

....

20___ ....

....

20___ ....

....

JAN
3

20___ ....

....

20___ ....

....

20___ ....

....

20___ ....

....

20___ ....

....

20___ ....

....

20___ ....

....

20___ ....

....

20___ ....

....

20___ ....

....

20___ ....

....

20___ ....

....

JAN 4

JAN 5

JAN 6

JAN 7

20__ ....
....
20__ ....
....
20__ ....
....

JAN 8

20__ ....
....
20__ ....
....
20__ ....
....

JAN 9

20__ ....
....
20__ ....
....
20__ ....
....

20 ___

20 ___

20 ___

20 ___

20 ___

20 ___

20 ___

20 ___

20 ___

JAN 10

JAN 11

JAN 12

JAN 13

20___ ....

....

20___ ....

....

20___ ....

....

JAN 14

20___ ....

....

20___ ....

....

20___ ....

....

JAN 15

20___ ....

....

20___ ....

....

20___ ....

....

20___ ....

20___ ....

20___ ....

20___ ....

20___ ....

20___ ....

20___ ....

20___ ....

20___ ....

JAN 19

20 _____

....

20 _____

....

20 _____

....

JAN 20

20 _____

....

20 _____

....

20 _____

....

JAN 21

20 _____

....

20 _____

....

20 _____

....

20___ ....

....

20___ ....

....

20___ ....

....

20___ ....

....

20___ ....

....

20___ ....

....

20___ ....

....

20___ ....

....

20___ ....

....

JAN 25

20___

20___

20___

JAN 26

20___

20___

20___

JAN 27

20___

20___

20___

20___ ....

20___ ....

20___ ....

20___ ....

20___ ....

20___ ....

20___ ....

20___ ....

20___ ....

JAN
28

JAN
29

JAN
30

JAN
31

20___ ....
....
20___ ....
....
20___ ....
....

"YOU CAN'T USE UP CREATIVITY. THE MORE YOU USE, THE MORE YOU HAVE."

—Maya Angelou

FEB 1

20___ ....
....
20___ ....
....
20___ ....
....

FEB 2

20___ ....
....
20___ ....
....
20___ ....
....

FEB 3

20___ ....
....
20___ ....
....
20___ ....
....

20___ ....

....

20___ ....

....

20___ ....

....

FEB 4

20___ ....

....

20___ ....

....

20___ ....

....

FEB 5

20___ ....

....

20___ ....

....

20___ ....

....

FEB 6

FEB 7

20___

....

20___

....

20___

....

FEB 8

20___

....

20___

....

20___

....

FEB 9

20___

....

20___

....

20___

....

20 ___

20 ___

20 ___

20 ___

20 ___

20 ___

FEB 10

FEB 11

FEB 12

FEB 13

20___ ....
....
20___ ....
....
20___ ....
....

FEB 14

20___ ....
....
20___ ....
....
20___ ....
....

FEB 15

20___ ....
....
20___ ....
....
20___ ....
....

20___ ....
....
20___ ....
....
20___ ....
....

FEB 16

20___ ....
....
20___ ....
....
20___ ....
....

FEB 17

20___ ....
....
20___ ....
....
20___ ....
....

FEB 18

FEB 19

20__ ....

20__ ....

20__ ....

FEB 20

20__ ....

20__ ....

20__ ....

FEB 21

20__ ....

20__ ....

20__ ....

20 ___ ....

....

20 ___ ....

....

20 ___ ....

....

20 ___ ....

....

20 ___ ....

....

20 ___ ....

....

20 ___ ....

....

20 ___ ....

....

20 ___ ....

....

20 ___ ....

....

FEB 25

20___ ....

....

20___ ....

....

20___ ....

....

FEB 26

20___ ....

....

20___ ....

....

20___ ....

....

FEB 27

20___ ....

....

20___ ....

....

20___ ....

....

20 ___ ....

....

20 ___ ....

....

20 ___ ....

....

20 ___ ....

....

20 ___ ....

....

20 ___ ....

....

"YOU CAN'T STOP THE WAVES, BUT YOU CAN LEARN TO SURF."

—Jon Kabat-Zinn

20 ___ ....
....

20 ___ ....
....

20 ___ ....
....

20 ___ ....
....

20 ___ ....
....

20 ___ ....
....

20 ___ ....
....

20 ___ ....
....

20 ___ ....
....

MAR 1

MAR 2

MAR 3

MAR 4

20 __

....

....

20 __

....

....

20 __

....

....

MAR 5

20 __

....

....

20 __

....

....

20 __

....

....

MAR 6

20 __

....

....

20 __

....

....

20 __

....

....

20__

20__

20__

20__

20__

20__

20__

20__

MAR 7

MAR 8

MAR 9

MAR 10

20___

20___

20___

MAR 11

20___

20___

20___

MAR 12

20___

20___

20___

20 ___

20 ___

20 ___

20 ___

20 ___

20 ___

20 ___

20 ___

20 ___

MAR
13

MAR
14

MAR
15

MAR 16

20___ ....

....

20___ ....

....

20___ ....

....

MAR 17

20___ ....

....

20___ ....

....

20___ ....

....

MAR 18

20___ ....

....

20___ ....

....

20___ ....

....

20 ___

20 ___

20 ___

20 ___

20 ___

20 ___

20 ___

20 ___

20 ___

MAR 22

20 ___ ....

....

20 ___ ....

....

20 ___ ....

....

MAR 23

20 ___ ....

....

20 ___ ....

....

20 ___ ....

....

MAR 24

20 ___ ....

....

20 ___ ....

....

20 ___ ....

....

20＿ ....

....

20＿ ....

....

20＿ ....

....

20＿ ....

....

20＿ ....

....

20＿ ....

....

20＿ ....

....

20＿ ....

....

20＿ ....

....

MAR 25

MAR 26

MAR 27

MAR 28

20___ ....

....

20___ ....

....

20___ ....

....

MAR 29

20___ ....

....

20___ ....

....

20___ ....

....

MAR 30

20___ ....

....

20___ ....

....

20___ ....

....

20 __ ....

....

20 __ ....

....

20 __ ....

....

MAR
31

"IF YOUR DREAMS DO NOT SCARE YOU, THEY ARE NOT BIG ENOUGH."

—Ellen Johnson Sirleaf

20___

20___

20___

20___

20___

20___

20___

20___

20___

APR 4

20___ ....
....
20___ ....
....
20___ ....
....

APR 5

20___ ....
....
20___ ....
....
20___ ....
....

APR 6

20___ ....
....
20___ ....
....
20___ ....
....

20___

20___

20___

20___

20___

20___

20___

20___

20___

APR 7

APR 8

APR 9

APR 10

20___
....
....
20___
....
....
20___
....
....

APR 11

20___
....
....
20___
....
....
20___
....
....

APR 12

20___
....
....
20___
....
....
20___
....
....

20___ ....

....

20___ ....

....

20___ ....

....

20___ ....

....

20___ ....

....

20___ ....

....

20___ ....

....

20___ ....

....

20___ ....

....

APR 13

APR 14

APR 15

41

APR 16

20___ ....
....
20___ ....
....
20___ ....
....

APR 17

20___ ....
....
20___ ....
....
20___ ....
....

APR 18

20___ ....
....
20___ ....
....
20___ ....
....

42

20___ ....

....

20___ ....

....

20___ ....

....

20___ ....

....

20___ ....

....

20___ ....

....

20___ ....

....

20___ ....

....

20___ ....

....

APR 22

APR 23

APR 24

20____

20____

20____

20____

20____

20____

20____

20____

20____

20___ ....

....

20___ ....

....

20___ ....

....

20___ ....

....

20___ ....

....

20___ ....

....

20___ ....

....

20___ ....

....

20___ ....

....

APR 25

APR 26

APR 27

APR 28

20___ ....
....
20___ ....
....
20___ ....
....

APR 29

20___ ....
....
20___ ....
....
20___ ....
....

APR 30

20___ ....
....
20___ ....
....
20___ ....
....

"THE GREATEST SECRETS ARE ALWAYS HIDDEN IN THE MOST UNLIKELY PLACES. THOSE WHO DON'T BELIEVE IN MAGIC WILL NEVER FIND IT."

—Roald Dahl

MAY 1

20___ ....
....
20___ ....
....
20___ ....
....

MAY 2

20___ ....
....
20___ ....
....
20___ ....
....

MAY 3

20___ ....
....
20___ ....
....
20___ ....
....

20 ___

20 ___

20 ___

20 ___

20 ___

20 ___

20 ___

20 ___

20 ___

MAY 4

MAY 5

MAY 6

MAY 7

20___

20___

20___

MAY 8

20___

20___

20___

MAY 9

20___

20___

20___

20___

20___

20___

20___

20___

20___

20___

20___

20___

MAY 10

MAY 11

MAY 12

MAY 13

20___ ....

20___ ....

20___ ....

MAY 14

20___ ....

20___ ....

20___ ....

MAY 15

20___ ....

20___ ....

20___ ....

20___

20___

20___

20___

20___

20___

20___

20___

20___

MAY 16

MAY 17

MAY 18

MAY 19

20___ ....

20___ ....

20___ ....

MAY 20

20___ ....

20___ ....

20___ ....

MAY 21

20___ ....

20___ ....

20___ ....

20___ ....

....

20___ ....

....

20___ ....

....

20___ ....

....

20___ ....

....

20___ ....

....

20___ ....

....

20___ ....

....

20___ ....

....

MAY
22

MAY
23

MAY
24

55

MAY 25

20___ ....
....
20___ ....
....
20___ ....
....

MAY 26

20___ ....
....
20___ ....
....
20___ ....
....

MAY 27

20___ ....
....
20___ ....
....
20___ ....
....

20 ___

20 ___

20 ___

20 ___

20 ___

20 ___

20 ___

20 ___

20 ___

MAY
28

MAY
29

MAY
30

MAY
31

20 _____ ....

....

20 _____ ....

....

20 _____ ....

....

"AT LEAST I KNOW WHO I WAS WHEN I GOT UP THIS MORNING, BUT I THINK I MUST HAVE BEEN CHANGED SEVERAL TIMES SINCE THEN."

—Lewis Carroll

JUN 1

20___ ....

....

20___ ....

....

20___ ....

....

JUN 2

20___ ....

....

20___ ....

....

20___ ....

....

JUN 3

20___ ....

....

20___ ....

....

20___ ....

....

20___ ....

....

20___ ....

....

20___ ....

....

20___ ....

....

20___ ....

....

20___ ....

....

20___ ....

....

20___ ....

....

20___ ....

....

JUN 4

JUN 5

JUN 6

JUN 7

20____ ....
....
20____ ....
....
20____ ....
....

JUN 8

20____ ....
....
20____ ....
....
20____ ....
....

JUN 9

20____ ....
....
20____ ....
....
20____ ....
....

20 ___ ....

20 ___ ....

20 ___ ....

20 ___ ....

20 ___ ....

20 ___ ....

20 ___ ....

20 ___ ....

20 ___ ....

JUN 13

20___

20___

20___

JUN 14

20___

20___

20___

JUN 15

20___

20___

20___

20___

20___

20___

20___

20___

20___

20___

20___

20___

JUN
16

JUN
17

JUN
18

JUN
19

20___ ....
....

20___ ....
....

20___ ....
....

20___ ....
....

20___ ....
....

JUN
20

20___ ....
....

20___ ....
....

JUN
21

20___ ....
....

20___ ....
....

20___ ....

....

20___ ....

....

20___ ....

....

20___ ....

....

20___ ....

....

20___ ....

....

20___ ....

....

20___ ....

....

20___ ....

....

JUN 22

JUN 23

JUN 24

JUN
25

20___ ....

....

20___ ....

....

20___ ....

....

JUN
26

20___ ....

....

20___ ....

....

20___ ....

....

JUN
27

20___ ....

....

20___ ....

....

20___ ....

....

20 ___ ....

20 ___ ....

20 ___ ....

20 ___ ....

20 ___ ....

20 ___ ....

20 ___ ....

20 ___ ....

20 ___ ....

"YOUR STORY IS WHAT YOU HAVE, WHAT YOU WILL ALWAYS HAVE. IT IS SOMETHING TO OWN."

—Michelle Obama

20___ ....

....

20___ ....

....

20___ ....

....

20___ ....

....

20___ ....

....

20___ ....

....

20___ ....

....

20___ ....

....

20___ ....

....

JUL 1

JUL 2

JUL 3

JUL 4

20___

20___

20___

JUL 5

20___

20___

20___

JUL 6

20___

20___

20___

20___

20___

20___

20___

20___

20___

20___

20___

20___

73

JUL 10

20__

20__

20__

JUL 11

20__

20__

20__

JUL 12

20__

20__

20__

20___ ....

....

20___ ....

....

20___ ....

....

20___ ....

....

20___ ....

....

20___ ....

....

20___ ....

....

20___ ....

....

20___ ....

....

JUL 16

20___ ....
....
20___ ....
....
20___ ....
....

JUL 17

20___ ....
....
20___ ....
....
20___ ....
....

JUL 18

20___ ....
....
20___ ....
....
20___ ....
....

20___ ....
....

20___ ....
....

20___ ....
....

20___ ....
....

20___ ....
....

20___ ....
....

20___ ....
....

20___ ....
....

20___ ....
....

JUL 19

JUL 20

JUL 21

JUL 22

20___ ....

....

20___ ....

....

20___ ....

....

JUL 23

20___ ....

....

20___ ....

....

20___ ....

....

JUL 24

20___ ....

....

20___ ....

....

20___ ....

....

20__ ....

....

20__ ....

....

20__ ....

....

20__ ....

....

20__ ....

....

20__ ....

....

20__ ....

....

20__ ....

....

20__ ....

....

JUL
25

JUL
26

JUL
27

JUL 28

20 ___

20 ___

20 ___

JUL 29

20 ___

20 ___

20 ___

JUL 30

20 ___

20 ___

20 ___

20 ___ ....
....

20 ___ ....
....

20 ___ ....
....

**JUL
31**

"OFTEN WHEN YOU THINK YOU'RE AT THE END OF SOMETHING, YOU'RE AT THE BEGINNING OF SOMETHING ELSE."

—Fred Rogers

20 ___

20 ___

20 ___

20 ___

20 ___

20 ___

20 ___

20 ___

20 ___

AUG 1

AUG 2

AUG 3

20 __

20 __

20 __

20 __

20 __

20 __

20 __

20 __

20 __

20___

20___

20___

20___

20___

20___

20___

20___

AUG 7

AUG 8

AUG 9

AUG 10

20___

20___

20___

AUG 11

20___

20___

20___

AUG 12

20___

20___

20___

20___ ....

20___ ....

20___ ....

20___ ....

20___ ....

20___ ....

20___ ....

20___ ....

20___ ....

AUG 13

AUG 14

AUG 15

*20*___

*20*___

*20*___

*20*___

*20*___

*20*___

*20*___

*20*___

*20*___

20 ___ ....

....

20 ___ ....

....

20 ___ ....

....

20 ___ ....

....

20 ___ ....

....

20 ___ ....

....

20 ___ ....

....

20 ___ ....

....

20 ___ ....

....

AUG 22

20＿ ....

....

20＿ ....

....

20＿ ....

....

AUG 23

20＿ ....

....

20＿ ....

....

20＿ ....

....

AUG 24

20＿ ....

....

20＿ ....

....

20＿ ....

....

90

20 __ ....
....
20 __ ....
....
20 __ ....
....
20 __ ....
....
20 __ ....
....
20 __ ....
....
20 __ ....
....
20 __ ....
....
20 __ ....
....

AUG 25

AUG 26

AUG 27

AUG 28

20 __ ....

....

20 __ ....

....

20 __ ....

....

AUG 29

20 __ ....

....

20 __ ....

....

20 __ ....

....

AUG 30

20 __ ....

....

20 __ ....

....

20 __ ....

....

20 ___

20 ___

AUG
31

20 ___

"YOU CANNOT SWIM FOR NEW HORIZONS UNTIL YOU HAVE COURAGE TO LOSE SIGHT OF THE SHORE."

—William Faulkner

20 ___ ....

20 ___ ....

20 ___ ....

20 ___ ....

20 ___ ....

20 ___ ....

20 ___ ....

20 ___ ....

20 ___ ....

SEP 1

SEP 2

SEP 3

SEP
4

20___

20___

20___

SEP
5

20___

20___

20___

SEP
6

20___

20___

20___

20___ ....

....

20___ ....

....

20___ ....

....

20___ ....

....

20___ ....

....

20___ ....

....

20___ ....

....

20___ ....

....

20___ ....

....

SEP 7

SEP 8

SEP 9

SEP 10

20___

20___

20___

SEP 11

20___

20___

20___

SEP 12

20___

20___

20___

20___

20___

20___

20___

20___

20___

20___

20___

20___

SEP 13

SEP 14

SEP 15

SEP 16

20___

20___

20___

SEP 17

20___

20___

20___

SEP 18

20___

20___

20___

20___ ....

....

20___ ....

....

20___ ....

....

20___ ....

....

20___ ....

....

20___ ....

....

20___ ....

....

20___ ....

....

20___ ....

....

SEP 19

SEP 20

SEP 21

SEP 22

20___ ....

....

20___ ....

....

20___ ....

....

SEP 23

20___ ....

....

20___ ....

....

20___ ....

....

SEP 24

20___ ....

....

20___ ....

....

20___ ....

....

20 _____ ....

20 _____ ....

20 _____ ....

20 _____ ....

20 _____ ....

20 _____ ....

20 _____ ....

20 _____ ....

20 _____ ....

SEP 25

SEP 26

SEP 27

SEP 28

20 __

20 __

20 __

SEP 29

20 __

20 __

20 __

SEP 30

20 __

20 __

20 __

"DON'T FORGET—NO ONE ELSE SEES THE WORLD THE WAY YOU DO, SO NO ONE ELSE CAN TELL THE STORIES THAT YOU HAVE TO TELL."

—Charles de Lint

OCT 1

20__

20__

20__

OCT 2

20__

20__

20__

OCT 3

20__

20__

20__

20___ ....

....

20___ ....

....

20___ ....

....

20___ ....

....

20___ ....

....

20___ ....

....

20___ ....

....

20___ ....

....

20___ ....

....

OCT 4

OCT 5

OCT 6

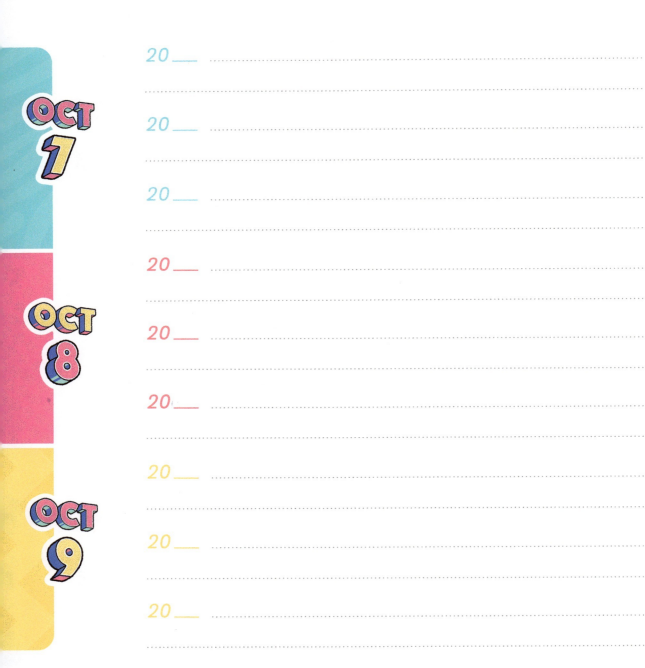

OCT 7

20___ ....
....
20___ ....
....
20___ ....
....

OCT 8

20___ ....
....
20___ ....
....
20___ ....
....

OCT 9

20___ ....
....
20___ ....
....
20___ ....
....

20___ ....

20___ ....

20___ ....

20___ ....

20___ ....

20___ ....

20___ ....

20___ ....

20___ ....

OCT 10

OCT 11

OCT 12

OCT 13

20___

20___

20___

OCT 14

20___

20___

20___

OCT 15

20___

20___

20___

20___

20___

20___

20___

20___

20___

20___

20___

20___

OCT
16

OCT
17

OCT
18

OCT 19

20 ___

20 ___

20 ___

OCT 20

20 ___

20 ___

20 ___

OCT 21

20 ___

20 ___

20 ___

20___

20___

20___

20___

20___

20___

20___

20___

20___

OCT
22

OCT
23

OCT
24

20___ ....
....

20___ ....
....

20___ ....
....

20___ ....
....

20___ ....
....

20___ ....
....

20___ ....
....

20___ ....
....

20___ ....
....

20___

20___

20___

20___

20___

20___

20___

20___

20___

OCT
28

OCT
29

OCT
30

115

OCT
31

*20*___

*20*___

*20*___

116

"I LIKE THE NIGHT. WITHOUT THE DARK, WE'D NEVER SEE THE STARS."

—Stephenie Meyer

NOV 1

20___
....
....

20___
....
....

20___
....
....

NOV 2

20___
....
....

20___
....
....

20___
....
....

NOV 3

20___
....
....

20___
....
....

20___
....
....

20___ ....

....

20___ ....

....

20___ ....

....

20___ ....

....

20___ ....

....

20___ ....

....

20___ ....

....

20___ ....

....

20___ ....

....

NOV 4

NOV 5

NOV 6

NOV 1

20___ ....
....
20___ ....
....
20___ ....
....

NOV 8

20___ ....
....
20___ ....
....
20___ ....
....

NOV 9

20___ ....
....
20___ ....
....
20___ ....
....

20___ ....

....

20___ ....

....

20___ ....

....

20___ ....

....

20___ ....

....

20___ ....

....

20___ ....

....

20___ ....

....

20___ ....

....

20___ ....

....

NOV 13

20___ ....

....

20___ ....

....

20___ ....

....

NOV 14

20___ ....

....

20___ ....

....

20___ ....

....

NOV 15

20___ ....

....

20___ ....

....

20___ ....

....

20__ ....

....

20__ ....

....

20__ ....

....

20__ ....

....

20__ ....

....

20__ ....

....

20__ ....

....

20__ ....

....

20__ ....

....

NOV 19

20 ___

20 ___

20 ___

NOV 20

20 ___

20 ___

20 ___

NOV 21

20 ___

20 ___

20 ___

20 _____ ....

....

20 _____ ....

....

20 _____ ....

....

20 _____ ....

....

20 _____ ....

....

20 _____ ....

....

20 _____ ....

....

20 _____ ....

....

NOV 22

NOV 23

NOV 24

125

NOV 25

20___ ....
....
20___ ....
....
20___ ....
....

NOV 26

20___ ....
....
20___ ....
....
20___ ....
....

NOV 27

20___ ....
....
20___ ....
....
20___ ....
....

20 __

20 __

20 __

20 __

20 __

20 __

20 __

20 __

20 __

"YOU CAN'T RUN AWAY FROM WHO YOU ARE, BUT WHAT YOU CAN DO IS RUN TOWARD WHO YOU WANT TO BE."

—Jason Reynolds

20___

20___

20___

20___

20___

20___

20___

20___

20___

DEC
1

DEC
2

DEC
3

DEC 4

20___

20___

20___

DEC 5

20___

20___

20___

DEC 6

20___

20___

20___

20 ___ ....

20 ___ ....

20 ___ ....

20 ___ ....

20 ___ ....

20 ___ ....

20 ___ ....

20 ___ ....

20 ___ ....

DEC
7

DEC
8

DEC
9

DEC 10

20 __ ....

....

20 __ ....

....

20 __ ....

....

DEC 11

20 __ ....

....

20 __ ....

....

20 __ ....

....

DEC 12

20 __ ....

....

20 __ ....

....

20 __ ....

....

20 ___

20 ___

20 ___

20 ___

20 ___

20 ___

20 ___

20 ___

20 ___

DEC 16

20___

20___

20___

DEC 17

20___

20___

20___

DEC 18

20___

20___

20___

20 __ ....

20 __ ....

20 __ ....

20 __ ....

20 __ ....

20 __ ....

20 __ ....

20 __ ....

20 __ ....

DEC 22

20___ ....
....
20___ ....
....
20___ ....
....

DEC 23

20___ ....
....
20___ ....
....
20___ ....
....

DEC 24

20___ ....
....
20___ ....
....
20___ ....
....

20 ___

20 ___

20 ___

20 ___

20 ___

20 ___

20 ___

20 ___

20 ___

20___ ....

....

20___ ....

....

20___ ....

....

20___ ....

....

20___ ....

....

20___ ....

....

20___ ....

....

20___ ....

....

20___ ....

....

20 ___ ....

....

20 ___ ....

....

20 ___ ....

....

DEC 31

"THE MOMENT YOU DOUBT WHETHER YOU CAN FLY, YOU CEASE FOR EVER TO BE ABLE TO DO IT."

—J. M. Barrie